Lois Anderson Leister

Sunlight

and

Shadows

by
Lois Anderson Leister

authorHOUSE™

1663 LIBERTY DRIVE, SUITE 200
BLOOMINGTON, INDIANA 47403
(800) 839-8640
WWW.AUTHORHOUSE.COM

First published by AuthorHouse 07/19/05

ISBN: 1-4208-5790-8 (sc)

Printed in the United States of America
Bloomington, Indiana

This book is printed on acid-free paper.

Dedication

To my children: Kathy, David, John, Joe, and Nancy who give me so much sunlight, and to my grandchildren: Tim, Michelle, Nikki, Greg, Liam, Zack, and Jenny who give me joy.

Table of Contents

JUST FOR FUN 105

SEASONS

Giant In The Basement

The wind careened around the house;
the room began to chill
as, creeping furtively, the cold
slipped in across the sill.
It edged the warmth back inch by inch,
a stealthy, stalking cat,
until grown over-bold, it pounced
upon the thermostat.
Then with a shudder of its skin,
a rumble in its womb,
the giant in the basement
puffed hot breath into the room.

Choices

I've seen it gather forces
with a white curl of its lip,
and hurl its shoulders to the sky
to burst against a ship,
or rolling from a silken trough
leap frothing at the shore
and fall away defeated
to build its strength once more.
It captures me in wonder
at its ever changing scene,
the fury of its thunder,
its silent, glassy green.
But I would take a mountain,
had I to make a choice,
where unseen creatures waken
at dawn to give it voice,
where rocky promontories
are heaped against the sky,
and trees grow perpendicular
with limbs that bend and sigh,
sometimes to shiver in the wind,
sometimes politely nod.
It seems to me a mountain
is reaching up to God.

Ribbon Road

I know a curling ribbon of a road,
dirt brown, and drifting lazy through the trees
to find an easy rise, the deepest shade,
and satisfied at serving little need
progress can justify.

A morning might see just one car pass by
to powder berry bushes on the bank;
truly a waste, berries cannot use
the taste of dust, but heaped upon the track,
it forms an inch of comfort to the toes.
It beckons one to linger through a wetting
to see first drops of rain make spatter holes.

I know a world-forgotten twist of road
that sends one trudging through a mile of winter
to see white stillness reaching out unbroken
beneath bone branches camouflaged in snow.
Something in me is needy of a road
that brings cathedral silence to the soul.

Sounds Of The Seasons

Spring brings laughter to the streets;
bird throats vibrate with delight;
cricket songs, and whippoorwills
liven up the night.

Summer wilts the thirsty soil;
lightning zigzags blinding bright;
every awesome thunder clap
knits startled bones up tight.

Crisping leaves proclaim the fall;
they brown and crush beneath the feet
as autumn winds begin to call,
and lure away the summer heat.

Winter takes fall's breath away,
incorporates it in a blow
that sweeps earth clean of yesterday,
and gift wraps it in silent snow.

Winter Wind

Birds are ruffled up for warmth;
star shaped gum leaves ride a draft,
diagonal, and come to rest
in huddled heaps against the house.

Branches are encased in glass;
puddles wear a frosted rim;
laden clouds begin to sift
particles of eiderdown.

Twilight comes before its time;
in the porch light's circled beam,
a host of exclamation points
toboggans tandem down the wind.

Tumbled together, each on each,
they heap and mound with artless grace,
until each bush and boundary fence
is incognito in a drift.

Wind On A Mountainside

The wind is dancing on the ground;
he's nudging at the stones,
and peeking under fallen leaves
with laughter in his tones.

When he collides with stolid trees,
That pay him little note,
he shakes and turns the giddy limbs,
a warning in his throat.

Then he attacks the mountainside,
and whining, turns about,
defeated by a barrier
whose strength has shut him out.

White Morning

On the tree nearest my window,
one lone branch lifts shoulders,
shivers itself free, and sends
an avalanche to thud weird markings
on the virgin snow beneath.
Through the muffled woods, a sigh
announces dawn and trees stretch to the sun.
Showers of powdered mist and clumps of white
track upon their own perfect carpets.
If I could hold this day in memory,
to view again, fresh with the wonder of a dawn,
I would not say that winter lasts too long.

Spring

The leaves are birthing;
yesterday they barely risked a nub
of brightness out to test the spring.
But O today, on promises of air,
suddenly grown braver than their roots,
they plunge, cautionless, to the sun.

Spring Transplant

My mind knows winter is not done,
and yet my heart grows light and merry
at one sun slanted June-like day
transplanted into February.

Wind Waiting

The wind is not content today
to hurry geese upon their southward flight;
he pirouettes with some untold delight,
and hints at secrets, only half in play.
Beware, his gusty murmur seems to say
to birds escaping in erratic flight;
they huddle now preparing for the night,
with heads tucked into feathered disarray.
When dawn arrives, they know without a doubt,
the secret that the wind held with such glee;
the muffled lanes and ermined branches show
what sent him into such an ecstasy.
He takes command, as with triumphant shout,
he towers drifts of freshly fallen snow.

My Mountain

My mountain climbs above a cloud,
reaching for the sun
to melt the frostbite from her spine
where icy winds have blown.
She balances upon a crest,
breathless as a prayer,
and then curves sharply to the west
to lean against the air
until grown bored with solitude,
she gives her trees a shake,
and plunging down a slide of shale,
goes wading in a lake.

Autumn Burning

The maples hold a charm for me
that other woodlands lack;
beneath their glowing canopy,
my dreams meander back
to Indian summer yesterdays,
when autumn blazed the sky
with color, and a smoky haze,
in whispers, told the eye
that out beyond my glory space,
my gold and crimson bed,
a farmer labored to erase
a summer that was dead.

Progress

Extended ribbons of cement
creep across the continent,
displacing fields where flowers bloomed,
and graves where loved ones were entombed,
where placid cattle chewed their cud,
and meadows overflowed with flood.

In some far pastures, cows still graze,
and flowers spread a purple haze;
the streams have found a distant bed,
as have the long-departed dead,
and we have ribbons of cement
tying up the continent.

SMALL VOICES

Grandma's Kitchen

When full of tears, bereft of song,
with winter stretching wet and long,
or when my deeds led to disgrace,
I sought my special hiding place.
Behind the stove, the cat and I
would, dozing, hear the men tramp by,
and smell the warm security
of field and barn. Then, finally,
after the talk of crops and rain,
the kitchen would grow still again,
and creeping out, I would be fed
on Grandma's love and fresh baked bread.

Daily Routine

My neighbor searched for dirt that didn't show
while I chased a dog,
rocked a frightened Johnny,
and washed Joe.

While she hung her laundry
in a neat and sparkling row,
I plucked the thorns from fingers seeking roses,
wiped noses, and washed Joe.

Then while Johnny struggled with his laces,
for some even untying shoes is slow;
I used a washcloth kept in kitchen spaces
to wash Joe.

After we had spilled our way through luncheon,
sanity-saving nap time coming on,
I just pretended Joseph wasn't dirty,
and I washed John.

The Last Cowboy

His Levi's hold no glory,
his guns are obsolete.
What once was thronged with longing boys
is now an empty street.

He has a real rope lariat;
all the boys envied that,
but now the brow is furrowed
beneath the Stetson hat.

The boots of shining leather,
once reigning so supreme,
are wobbly reminders
of a sadly faded dream.

His laughing eyes are lonely;
there are sighs he can't control,
the only cowboy on the block,
the rest are Space Patrol.

A Son Enlists

I stored his clothes and cleaned the room,
removing every trace
of eighteen years with mop and broom;
but still I see his face.
He tried to look so confident.
Although I felt no joy,
I let him think I was content
to send away my boy.

I tried to teach him how to stand
alone, erect; today,
he did not need my helping hand
to turn and walk away.
But one would think, with eighteen years,
I would have taken one
to teach myself to conquer fears
and live without my son.

Security Check

Bare feet are silent on the floor;
muscles draw tight, the room is chill;
my light outlines the bedroom door;
a child cried, but now is still.
Silently I tour each room,
carefully move a wayward toy
across my path as in the gloom,
I mark the figure of each boy.
No trouble here, suddenly warm,
I gently draw the covers tight
around each sprawling, heedless form,
and tiptoe on across the night
to blanket daughters, safe asleep.
The baby, humped against the cold,
warms to a limp and boneless heap,
while I, a miser, count my gold.

Two-Fold

He climbed the high chair by himself
and I attached the tray.
I measured out the medicine,
and heard his small voice say,
"Ooh! My head is falling off!"
His small hands clutched his head.
"Ooh! I'd better hold it on!"
my frightened baby said.

Somehow, it seemed that I could see
the source of blinding pain,
the flashing sparks and misfires,
in the circuits of his brain.
We waited for the storm to pass
while danger danced around;
both of us were paralyzed;
we screamed without a sound.

"Little One, take the medicine."
(It spills, my hand is shaking,
to keep your head from falling off,
to keep my heart from breaking.)

Night Thoughts

Dear Lord, I've checked on all the beds
to snug my children from the cold.
Last night, my sleep was torn to shreds;
I am too young to feel so old.

Could baby slumber through the night
without demanding to be fed,
and no small boy announce his plight
with, "Mommy, I just wet my bed!"?

Lord, may this night its silence keep,
for more than just an hour or two,
without a, "Mommy, I can't sleep;
can I get into bed with you"?

But that was many years ago.
This night is stiller than a sigh;
the moon is creeping cold and low.
My memories ride high.

Each silent room, I've tiptoed through,
but no small head is pillowed there;
I keep a lonely rendezvous
with my forsaken rocking chair.

Caution Please

Little one who climbs the highest,
runs atop the wall,
leaps across the greatest distance
heedless of a fall,
would that you could bear a tether,
life is not so free;
do not rush to fast for breathing,
stay awhile with me.

Dawn Discovery

Santa is left without a ho;
the Easter Bunny exits hopping;
my mantle never more may know
the resurrected Christmas stocking.
Magic fades before the truth
in eyes grown newly wiser, wary;
a pillow just revealed a tooth
that was not ransomed by a fairy.

Prolifically Speaking

How very many prayers I said;
in each, repeatedly,
I asked my fervent, heartfelt wish:
a baby please, for me.
Now I've a strong suspicion
the Lord is having fun
answering my many prayers,
One . . . by . . . one . . . by . . . one.

Baby Feet

My baby lurches drunkenly
on chubby feet still soft and round;
he thinks they're made for walking;
they are more for kissing, I have found.
But he has dreams of floor and street,
and must be up and on his way.
Stagger, stumble little feet;
I shall kiss you more today.

First Child – First Day Of School

My need of you before your birth
was more than poet tongue can say.
Although six years have held your face,
my need is still the same today.
I am so big and you so small,
you think that only you can fear,
or grieve at parting for a day,
and tremble as the hour draws near.
But you must pass beyond my reach,
and if I keep my courage true,
you will not know your need of me
is nothing to my need of you.

Fourth Child – First Day Of School

Firmly pushed before my hand
is nine parts cleanliness,
one part dirt I missed somehow,
five parts laughter,
two parts tears,
one part stubbornness,
two parts noise,
a pinch of disobedience,
a dash of eagerness to please
spiced strongly with imagination.
He is my son, still mine for prayers,
scoldings and kisses, still beloved,
but yours now five days a week!
Thank God!

Lois Anderson Leister

Middle Child

When I was sick,
I saw my programs on TV,
with two large pillows back of me,
and drank hot lemonade,
and soup in a cup, and mother made
time for checkers, and telling why,
and walking softly, and smiling by.
I think tomorrow I may be
sick again so I can see
how noticing everyone is of me.

Daughter, Come Home!

I'm stranded with a healthy man,
and three loud, lusty boys;
not another quartet
can equal them for noise.
There are no bobby-pins about,
no curlers in a chair;
the bathroom is not blossomed out
with frilly underwear.
There is no one to comfort me,
to share my isolation,
or break this male monopoly;
my daughter's on vacation.

The Golden Hour

There is a silence strangely rare,
more meaningful than all words spoken,
that fills the first delightful hour,
after the TV is broken.

Haiku

drunken bicycle
staggers down summer street
a child's first solo

If For Mothers

If I didn't have two babies to feed,
the oldest one's homework to check,
and to see that another is scrubbed free of dirt,
with both his ears minus a peck,
if, all at one time, my floors were dust free,
the creeper devours each speck,
if there weren't a mountain of mending to do,
and the magazine rack such a wreck,
with bushels of laundry to sort, wash, and fold,
they are such a pain in the neck!
I'd be so full of energy, what I would do,
is have me a baby, by heck!

Procrastination

Yesterday I would have worked,
it's what I planned to do,
but a little boy was fevered,
so we rocked the morning through.

The day before, I meant to clean,
but baby is too young
to play outdoors unsupervised;
growing things need the sun.

So I trimmed the hedges,
weeded a flower bed,
got myself exhausted
and took a nap instead.

Today my house is such a mess
it couldn't get much worse,
and looking at it tires me;
that's why I write this verse.

VISIONS

Canvas Castle

My camping trailer, squat and wide,
unprepossessing in its size,
trails mindlessly behind the car;
it is a kingdom in disguise.

When we preempt a forest plot,
nature's creatures slip away
to ring a cautious no-man's-land;
only the humming insects stay.

But from each fronded bush and tree,
shy eyes peer out in mute surprise,
as from a square ungainly box,
they see my canvas castle rise.

No Space Like Home

They say that it will not take long
to colonize the moon,
and with our population growth,
it cannot be too soon.
The earth has been camped out, they say,
with no more wilderness;
the new frontier's the latest word,
but unless I miss my guess,
when campers cry,
"The moon or bust!"
I'll be pitching my tent
on earthly dust.

Campomania

A camper is a person who,
five days a week, contributes to
civilization's progress march,
with structured steel and concrete arch,
with huge machines that belch and roar,
and spew cement on nature's floor.
But when the weekend rolls around,
a camper is the guy who's found
with trailer, motorhome, and tent,
rushing to where the forest went.

Missing Emily

Does no one write in rhyme today,
in words that swell the rhythm of the heart,
and form a shape a dream can hold?

Emily was born with magic, singing thoughts,
and almost-rhymes that steeped the soul
with wistfulness and dreaming.

Free verse is tennis with no net,
to paraphrase word singer Robert Frost,
who also knew the magic of the rhyme.

Kittanning

My town is nested down in sudden hills
that drop to meet the sweeping Allegheny
in startling descent; there is no road
that finds an easy entry from the slopes,
and no thought given to timid souls
fearful of swinging unexpected curves.

Somewhere, on rocky ledges west of town,
my roots still cling. Although I took
my life to other streets in other towns,
a part of me still blossoms in the clay.

Awareness

If you but touch me passing by,
you will become a part of me.
I am flavored by your sigh;
your laughter sets my singing free.
There is no touch so light that I
can bear, and unaffected be;
if you but touch me, passing by,
you will become a part of me.
So if my fainting soul grows shy,
and hesitates before your plea,
I offer you no alibi
except that, irreversibly,
if you but touch me passing by,
you will become a part of me.

The Flight Of Apollo 8

Breath held, I watched the capsule leave the earth,
forgotten Christmas garlands in my hands.
I could not reconstruct the Christ Child's birth
two thousand years ago in Bible lands,
or link it now with weird unfathomed sands,
and craters ringed about with lunar dust.
My sorrow over Herod's cruel commands
diminished as I viewed the moon's gray crust.
With trembling heart, I watched as three men thrust
their lives into God's keeping out in space.
I failed to see a testament of trust
and faith in him in that imperiled place.
Then, from three-hundred-thousand miles, a prayer!
An astronaut breathed God into the air.

Chancellorsville

I shiver in the shadows
of the ghosts upon the ground;
my breath is caged within me
as I listen for the sound
of twigs beneath the broken shoes,
the whisper of the wool,
as it slithers in the grasses,
with each body-heaving pull
of the elbows, as the soldiers
creep in writhing, jagged lines,
on the left through high grass pastures,
on the right, Virginia Pines.

Are they Blue? It does not matter;
are they Gray? I do not care.
They are met, and I am witness
to the thousands dying there.

I can hear the bugles sounding,
and the belching cannon's boom;
they are screaming all about me
in the smoke infested gloom.
They are falling all about me,
and the dusty grass grows red;
I see grisly death contortions
of a boy without a head.
Now the silence drops forever
on the Blue and Gray; my pain
is for all the nation's children;
they are mine and they are slain.

To My Parents

It seems so very strange that I
can write of trees and birds,
and astronauts, and ESP,
but I can't find the words
to say how proud I am of you.
Your love has nourished me
from birth till now, and if it seems
I treat time heedlessly,
don't be deceived. If I could have
ten decades and a day
to share with you, I would not give
one hour of it away.

Tuesday

If I lose my mind it will be Tuesday,
when grief like mountains sits upon my heart,
and all inside my head the gray thought islands
are washed by pain. If I fall apart
it will be with old wounds freshly opened,
the bloody gashes raw and lying bare,
that I had learned to live with, so familiar
that sometimes I could think they were not there.
But if I live through Tuesday, not in pieces,
though all the world is hopeless, barren, bleak,
in ragged, tattered remnants of my courage,
I think I will survive another week.

The Ballad Of Pioneer Woman

When woman walked the wagon track
where few had gone before,
her home and comfort on her back,
a nation to explore.

She left her table for a stump,
her washtub for a stream;
each foot became an aching lump,
her nourishment a dream.

She lived with nature in her hand,
and where the cedars sigh,
she gained an essence of the land
the sheltered could not buy.

The years have swept the trails away,
and civilized the earth,
but woman keeps alive today
her heritage of birth.

As long as mountains rim the skies,
the pioneer remains
with far-off places in her eyes,
and camping in her veins.

Mountain Woman
(To my mother—eighty years old)

Rocks to me are to be wondered at,
respected, sat upon or walked on,
careful not to stumble over.

Rocks to her are challenges;
but rocks do not believe disaster comes
from five-foot grandmothers.

Bowed beneath her pry-bar and a sledge,
she contemplates her victim, sets her back,
and piece-by-piece divides the stone.

Some defeated armies line a drive,
while others form a drainage ditch
to give direction to the cast-off storm.

Now, where rocks once reigned in stolid might,
phylox and ivy creep; I've seen her push
a mountain back to make a garden place.

The Ballad Of The Brothers

Rising in power to lead a great nation,
handsome as deities, richer than kings,
none is untouched by the fate of the brothers;
sad is the ballad a grieved nation sings.

Shrouded in infamy, tragedy, glory,
destined for legend, the Kennedy name,
Ted took a life and Jack rescued many;
Bobby did neither, but died just the same.

Both Jack and Bobby were struck down by killers;
a nation stands shamed by the cold, silent biers;
Ted must remember, with grief unremitting,
the chapter he fashioned in blood flavored tears.

Shaping the visions of seers and the sages,
brilliant and vigorous, spellbinding all,
the pages they wrote will not blur with the ages,
the aura of wonder, the thunderous fall.

Canyons

You hold your head lamenting too much peace.
Hope is a trap; it will be snatched away.
Retreat into the safety of your gloom;
reject my cheer; it is anathema to you.
Regretfully, I place my sunlit words,
upon the heap of unvoiced arguments
discarded through the years.

Sometimes, when trouble comes,
my mind defies imprisoned silence;
"When we get through this . . ." I start,
but words fall into canyons when you shout,
"I don't know why we try! It's just no use!"
Only my sigh proclaims the unsaid words
slipping from my lips backward to my brain.
They join the circled echoes where your shout
is trapped in bridgeless canyons of my mind.

Silence

Your thoughts reach out from shadowed halls;
I am so open to your reaching,
that all my self-protective walls
disintegrate, preclude the breeching.

So surely do I hear the voice
of your embattled spirit weeping,
that neither of us has a choice;
your grief is destined to my keeping.

Why is it then that I should know
your darkest depths, your soul's despairing,
who cannot shield you from a blow,
or ease your burden with my caring?

Others might seek a cold escape,
and leave such thoughts ignored, unspoken;
but I cannot rebuild the shape
of silence that your need has broken.

Precognition

Outside my mind, outside the shell
that houses blood and bone of me,
I dwelt an eon and a day,
or just a moment, who could tell?
Not I, who could not change the way,
or pull back from the agony.

I witnessed impact's upward heave
of legs and arms and twisted steel;
then scarred by shock, and doom foretold,
I stumbled back to join my soul.

I knew whose fate had been revealed,
and should I pray, and shout, and plead,
I could not halt approaching death,
delay or change that rendezvous.

Silent, I waved them through the door
upon a journey to the grave,
and waited, steeped in misery,
while they consumed, all unaware,
the hours till they caught up with me.

Because I Care

I hear the voice of your despair;
my eyes bleed crystal answers on the page.
I can't swim your sea, but if you lie
washing exhausted with the tide,
I will reach my hand to bring you
through the shallows to the shore.

Winging Words

Minds are solitary cells;
silence builds the walls
ungated, sightless, all the way
up to insanity.
It is the strength of winging words
refusing to be caged,
that crumbles prisons stone-on-stone,
and makes man viable.

SOUL SINGING

The Vigil

When God is folded close about your bed
to take your soul into his holy light,
too earthbound to behold where you are led,
I will not be a witness to the sight.
But I will share your final moments here,
and if the time is painful while we wait,
my arms will offer comfort, draw you near,
and I will pray for you and meditate.
When the time has come for your release,
I will know that Jesus is nearby.
When at last you rest and breathing cease,
perhaps I'll touch your face and softly cry.
But I will not be overcome by gloom,
if Jesus comes while I am in the room.

Look At Peter

There was a man who rowed with God,
and fished, and walked, and chatted at his side,
yet when they asked him if he knew the man,
shaken with fear and cowardice, he lied.

When, in the final moment courage came,
and he at last was master of his fear,
he flailed his sword about so futilely,
his only victim was a soldier's ear.

Thus through the centuries a trust has come
to all this weak and foolish race of men;
all that God asks of anyone is try,
and fall and rise, and fall and rise again.

Prayer For My Son

This is my son, while he is small,
I hold his hand that he may grow
safely protected from a fall.
Lord, guide his feet, he stumbles so.

When my small boy becomes a man,
his heart must take the bumps I know;
Lord, give him strength and courage then
so every knock and bump won't show.

And should his way be rough and long,
Lord, take his hand and let him know
when sudden twists may turn him wrong,
you'll guide his feet, he stumbles so.

Witness

I see a star descending
a banister of sky;
I hear an ocean thunder,
and unseen breezes sigh;
I feel an unborn baby
lift to life; and it is odd
that somewhere other witnesses
deny there is a God.

Hope Song

Hope sings a song inside my breast;
it lifts on fluttered wings.
If all the souls who feel depressed
could hear the song it sings
they, too, would stretch the sagging tips
of wings grown stiff and chill,
and soar from earthbound landing strips
to heaven's windowsill.

Soul Eyes

My soul has eyes but can't see snow,
or soft-blown spring, or autumns glow.
With other eyes I see all this;
but there is much that I would miss
without soul eyes; with these I know
eternity, and dreams, and so
thank you Lord, for giving me
two pairs of eyes with which to see.

A Time of Weeping

Without a time of suffering,
a soul would never know
how fatally another
can be shattered by a blow;
it takes a time of weeping
for wisdom roots to grow;
it is from barren sands of loss,
compassion rivers flow.

A Mother's Prayer

Lord, give me wisdom now to guide
their feet, but not to pull or shove;
give me the strength to quiet pride,
and not to smother them with love.
When they have traveled childhood's mile
and must walk tall without my touch,
Lord, give me courage then to smile,
and not to show it hurts so much.

Jesus To Me

You are my nourishment;
I draw on you as from beloved hills;
I find my strength in shadowed lanes,
in soft mist-hidden dawns,
in scrub grass hilltops, pungent
furrowed fields, in piney woods
brown-layered with a century of needles.
You have created these—my sustenance,
and you sustain me now.

Soul Cleaning

My soul became so cluttered
that finally I found
me squeezed into the center
with no room to turn around.

Heaped about on every side,
stacked along the wall,
were failures and embarrassments,
I hated to recall.

Standing, somehow each alone,
were hearts and souls and such
that had a chance to love me well,
but hadn't loved me much.

When I really looked at them,
in dreading and in doubt,
I found they were such silly things
that I could laugh them out.

Now I have a shining room,
and you outside my door,
come in, come in, I welcome you,
to dance upon the floor.

Communion

Last night as I was saying habit prayers,
God came, and I in ignorance,
attributed him but to be a flight
of fancy, visionary dreams, and he
knowing my great uncertainty and doubt,
in sadness said, "Have I created you?"
My startled mind was frozen mute with shock
until he said, "I am ashamed of you!"
Then my pride arose to shame me more,
and hardly bothering to hide
behind a civil tone, I asked, " Why me?"
My unvoiced outrage shouted to the air;
Why pick on me? Pick on one who kills or steals.
Are not these wrongs greater than mine?

My Lord began to fade away from me,
and suddenly forsaken by my pride,
my soul cried out, "Help me! I need you, Lord."
He stopped, and smiling, he drew near once more.

Shorn of my pride, and longing now to please,
I asked, "What would you have me do?"
My Lord, seeing the coming day beyond my sight,
said with a smile. "One thing I ask of you."
Tomorrow in the clear edged light,
doubt not I came." And with these words
He left me to my wonder and my joy.

71

The Pessimist And The Optimist

The sky is gray and the sun won't shine;
I'm sick and tired of winter skies.
The clouds sit on the mountain's spine;
I want it to be otherwise;

It feels and smells and looks like snow.
This is a day that isn't fit
for man or beast. I think I'll go
to my recliner chair and sit.

- - - - - - - - -

The sky is gray, the clouds are low.
I think it is a hopeful sign
that soon it might begin to snow
and decorate the mountain's spine.

Perhaps, I'll see some children fly
on sleds and snowboards down the hill,
and I will cheer as they pass by.
If I am asked to play, I will.

Prayer For Courage

The suffering I knew before
was all my little soul could stand.
I did not feel the challenge then
or know that triumph over pain
could lift the soul, enlarge, expand.
But I have learned a little now
of how your being fills the soul,
and I am greedy; I must stretch
my soul to gain its farthest reach;
I long to hold your being whole.
So help me bear, Lord, I implore,
my loss and pain courageously,
that when I stand before your throne,
my soul, its final fraction grown,
you may find all room in me.

In Rebuttal Of Praise

Do not judge me wise, or good,
godly, or kind. If I possess
some measure of these attributes,
it is but half of what I am.
Each value has an opposite,
and in one being both exist,
faults of the virtues. I can stoop
to depths as far as I can climb.
But if you say that I love much,
the only truth that I can claim;
it will suffice though I should rise
into some strange near-holiness.
It will suffice if I should fling
all moral values to the wind,
fumbling, stumbling, plunging down
to sink beneath my origin.

When Mother Died

Grief was jagged ice in me,
sharp edged and deadly cold;
I told myself that she was ill,
I said that she was old.

My mind was trapped in platitudes
that did not break the spell,
or free me the icy grip,
inside my brittle shell.

There were no words to comfort me,
no strength on which to draw,
until God circled me with love.
Warmth causes ice to thaw.

Absent Physician

My skin was wrapped about a pain
that beat relentlessly;
it tossed my frame from side to side,
without consulting me.

But Jesus stood beside my bed,
and promised to remain.
I wrapped my soul about his knees,
and joy transcended pain.

Last night the agony came back
to rule beneath my skin;
but worse to bear was emptiness,
where Jesus once had been.

God's Carpet

My eyes are not selective;
when I look at the stars,
I can't locate Orion
or Jupiter or Mars.

But I can find the milky way,
that sparkles in and out,
and if my faith should falter,
or tremble on a doubt,

I need but see that whited path
between me and the dawn,
that lovely starlit carpet
that Jesus walks upon.

Shadows

I watched my earthly shadow
an hour after noon,
and knew that it would surely grow;
it would be bigger soon.

My soul is just a shadow
of what it ought to be;
Lord, work my clay and help me grow;
spread your light in me.

Haiku

holy hush of death
a joyful soul is singing
butterfly set free

When This Is Done

There is a place in me where God still lives,
and dreams still rise; there is poetry,
and it will sing its way across the page
in joyful tribute to the world
once more, when this is done.

These things I know; the core of me
is more than grief and more than pain;
it will survive, captor and captive,
my unconquered soul.

LOVE LINES

When You Think Of Me

I cannot read your mind, but if my heart
lightens like ripened wheat fields when a breeze
ruffles grain and feathers clouds apart;
if, of a sudden, all my pressures ease,
and I am wheat in sunlight, fields aglow,
it does not matter that I cannot see
your face or hear your voice; somehow I know
that I am in your thoughts. This alchemy
does not employ a mystic sign or star,
a homing signal from a distant sphere,
or beam to guide my soul to where you are
each time your thoughts reach out to draw me near.
Yet if, in thundered moments, you should call,
I would hear you though stars and mountains fall.

The Choice

A dozen men just waited round
to heed my beck and call;
one flick of my pink fingertip
would galvanize them all.

Why was it, with a dozen men,
you were the one I chose?
You were the only one, my dear,
with marriage to propose.

Give Away

I told the world I loved him;
how I caroled to the sky!
My eyes said I adored him
to every passerby.

She told them all I lost him,
though she didn't say a thing;
she merely wore her own sure smile,
and his engagement ring.

When All Else Is Dust

The thoughts that I have captured with my pen
reside in books today, and it may be
that they will live to sing my dreams again
in some far land, some distant century.
My poems tell about my love for you,
a record of the rapture and the pain.
When my moment on this earth is through,
and all else dies with me, they may remain.
I wonder, are these verses truly mine?
Had you not carved your magic on my heart,
my written words, shaped to a new design,
would have another meaning to impart.
Although the world attributes them to me,
my verses tell of your complicity.

Heart Sonnet

Unsuspecting heart, you found a spring
that was not ever meant for you to know.
You found another soul to make you sing,
another heart to warm you in its glow.
But passing time leaves just a memory,
and spring has faded into summer now;
where once the mint green leaf buds used to be,
the fruit is forming clusters on the bough.
Hindsight decrees that I should build a wall,
and fasten you inside it with a chain
in case a sudden meeting or a call
should plunge you into springtime once again.
O foolish heart, if you should hear his laughter,
I think you'd climb a wall to follow after.

Phantom

Today I allowed my heart to remember,
to sort out the past—the spark from the ember.
There did I find you, still shrouded in pain,
but only a phantom, a grief on the wane.
What once held my heart a slave to command
has crumbled apart like dust in my hand.

Beyond

I've traveled past the sudden heart,
the stop-still panic of your name,
the bursting, shower-stinging start
of all my senses. I am tame
beyond all aching, and your tread
is not earth shaking; I am dead.

The Lover

He loved a lawn sun-dappled,
soft drip-dripping rain,
people Sunday chapeled,
a frosted windowpane;
he loved to see a kitten curled,
and here's the tragedy,
he loved the whole distracting world
as much as he loved me.

Candle Logic

To burn your candle at both ends,
there is one thing I learned,
you must hold on to the middle, friends.
That's how I got burned.

Graveyard Of Dreams

Last night I walked a quiet plot
where visions lay at rest;
I hurried past a tear stained spot
where loving failed the test
of being loved; I skipped the place
where daydreams cast aside,
were huddled in a brambled space,
forgotten where they died.
I passed unhesitatingly
where dreams lay in a tomb;
they were not worth the energy
required to make them bloom.
I did not like that shadowed way,
the dead aisles of pre-dawn,
I will return again today,
and plow it with a song.

Miracles

Beneath the gentle reaching of your mind,
your tender, caring sensitivity,
I find my soul resurgent, unresigned
to cautious sheltering; you open me.
You beckon to my timid soul, be free
and I begin to blossom and to grow,
responsive to a special empathy
that reassures and warms me in its glow.
I find capacities I did not know,
existing dormant, waking to a touch;
one would not think that love could change me so;
it is a miracle to feel so much.
And should you leave me bleeding, broken, lost,
for miracles, I would not count the cost.

Tomorrow

When I love you is just a phrase
we uttered in the past,
and time dissolves the golden haze
of dreams not meant to last,
I will remember how the touch
of eyes, joined for a minute,
could set me trembling, and how much
there was of magic in it.

Fallacy

There's no such thing as dead love;
I know that grief can ease,
but just the slanting of a head
can rouse your memories.
An echoing of laughter
through a mist of morning rain
can send you surging backward
into agonizing pain.

Second Thoughts

I saw my first love yesterday
and had a second look;
it is to my regret, I say
I saw my first love yesterday,
resembling a worn cliché.
O, what a jolt my dreaming took!
I saw my first love yesterday,
and had a second look.

I wish that I had passed him by
without a second glance;
my dreams fell flatter than a sigh;
I wish that I had passed him by.
Now I suppose I'll have to try
to find a new romance.
I wish that I had passed him by
without a second glance.

Fatalist

When he first left me
so shattered was I,
with my life all in ruins,
I wanted to die.
But the car wouldn't hit me;
the train didn't wreck;
the fall down the stairs
only stiffened my neck.
I failed to get sick
when I walked in the rain,
so I lived after all,
and got happy again.

Today

Today will be my gift to you;
you will not see me cry,
and nothing that I say or do
will let you know that I
am full of grief, and too aware
how little time is left.
I have learned how much I care
and soon alone, bereft,
I must begin to build again.
But for this precious day,
I'll laugh, there will be time for pain,
when you have gone away.

Your Words

Your words struck such a deadly blow,
I wondered that you did not know.
But blessedly, paralysis
congealed my face to nothingness.
It gave me time to summon pride
to hide the naked death inside;
behind a cloak of dignity,
I looked at what was left of me;
when I unclenched a rigored hand,
all my dreams slipped through like sand.

Retrospect

What dealt such bitter pain to me
in that long yesterday,
became a shadowed memory,
slipping its silent way.
The pain now blooming in my breast,
tomorrow can't hold sway.
Although this is the sharpest test
my soul is called upon,
it, too, will pass like all the rest
if I survive the dawn.

Private Funeral

There was no thing I could not be,
had I his love for company,
to cheer me on, to help me rise
beyond the scope of earthbound eyes.
But, careless of my soul's romance,
he hurried on, ignored the chance.
I could not, in my pride, insist
or even tell him what he missed.
So I laid my dreams to rest
where other dreams had failed the test.

Limbo

How could I have cared so much,
and been so young, so new,
that just a sentence was enough
to shatter me in two?

How was it that I soared on wings
to tremble on a star
and shimmer breathless at a touch;
how did I fall so far?

In a bereft and barren shell,
survivor of the pain,
I wonder what I would be like
if I could feel again.

Heart's Attic

This is a day postponed by dread;
today my heart begins
to free the shadowy corners
of spidery might-have-beens.

It's time to dust forgotten rooms
where whispery old ghosts play
games of never quite hide-and-seek
and just-about-gone-away.

Heartbreaks float in a hidden vial,
preserved in a brine of tears,
cradled on yesterday's memories;
they haven't been opened for years.

Heart, work carefully, quietly
with a duster of feathered prayer,
poised on a moment to run away
if someone is living there.

JUST FOR FUN

Time Lines

The golden age has lost its glow;
my teeth are laughing in a jar;
my aching joints are moving slow,
and when they move don't take me far.

My hair is floating down the drain;
I shower holding to a bar,
and all the parts that used to pain
are designated by a scar.

New lines have overrun my face,
and loss of mind is hard to bear;
I know that I should go someplace;
I wish I could remember where.

Dreams Of A Not-So-Great Poet

When I wrote verse at twenty-one,
my words were passion bred;
I thought that I could say a lot
that hadn't yet been said.

At forty, with perspective gained,
I knew that all was folly;
when poking fun at twenty-one,
the words I wrote were jolly.

But now that sixty has arrived,
I take a wistful note;
it would be fine to write a line
that someone else would quote.

Daisy

My Daisy came last,
the runt of the lot,
but ballots were cast
and that's what I got.
Little she stayed
while other dogs grew,
and little she played,
and little she knew,
except that she loved me,
and loved me a lot,
and when she had fleas,
well, that's what I got.
The fleas also loved me,
and loved me a lot.

The Rat Killers

A couple once lived in a house.
My story is quite sad.
They set the traps for roach and mouse,
but rats! That made them mad!

Once, barefoot in the bathroom,
this old man saw a rat,
"Old Woman, go and get the broom!"
he cried from where he sat.

"We'll get this creature, Wife," he said.
He used the broom to strike it.
The rat leaped right into the tub
because he didn't like it.

"I've got you now," the old man cried,
and struck a mighty blow.
The rat leaped out onto the floor,
and with a startled, "OH!

The man, himself, leaped in the tub
with both bare feet in motion.
He watched the rat from where he stood,
and had another notion.

"Wife, I will chase the rat your way;
you hit him with the door,
and if not dead, he'll surely fall
unconscious on the floor."

He chased the rat out through the door.
(But sometimes good plans fail.)
Her timing was a second off.
She trapped him by his tail.

The rat was trapped outside the room,
the man was trapped within.
"You kill him, Wife, he's on your side."
He shouted with a grin.

I do not like this plan, she thought;
the rat thought, *nor do I.*
"I think I'd rather hit the man,"
she muttered with a sigh.

She got her iron skillet out
and hit the hairy head.
"You can come out now, Husband.
The rat is dead," she said.

My Cat

Once, I was owned by a cat,
who seldom allowed me to pat
her sinuous side.
Sometimes when I tried,
her hair rose in spikes, and she spat.

But sometimes she'd lie at my side,
and shiver her soft, silky hide.
Then I'd fondle her fur;
she would stretch out and purr,
but if I said I owned her, I lied.

The Camel

Comfort is something camels lack.
When you sit upon one's back,
he kneels until you get astride
his flea-infested hairy hide.
The camel rises, back end first.
Your innards plummet, almost burst.
Your grip him tightly with each thigh
before his front lifts toward the sky.
A seat upon a camel's hump
is quite unsuited to a rump.

The Centipede

A creature that I can't abide
is the obnoxious centipede.
I hate the fragile, brittle hide
that hides the gooey stuff inside.

Into my house, I've seen him come,
his legs all keeping time;
he marches to some secret drum
or soldier's cadence rhyme.

I'd like to kill him, if I dared,
but I show him the door;
I'd stomp him if I weren't scared
he'd leave his goo upon my floor.

A Hare Raising Tale

A rabbit came calling one day,
He was dear in a floppy-eared way.
He played on the lawn,
and when he was gone
I was sad. I had hoped he would stay.

Ten rabbits came the next day.
They didn't come only to play.
They dined on my corn
on that fresh, dewy morn.
I threw rocks to drive them away.

Twenty rabbits came out of the mist
the next day. I said, "You insist
my garden to loot".
So I started to shoot.
I shot at twenty rabbits and missed.

The Disgrace of Hiram Itchey

It was upon that very day
and hour in Frederick town,
while Barbara Frietchie had her say
and harvested renown;

that Hiram Itchey walked the street,
and heard her window lifted;
but Itchey could not catch her words
because the wind had shifted.

Never one to be so rude
as to ignore her pleas,
he climbed a nearby flagpole
that wobbled in the breeze.

There he heard her very words
that have immortal grown,
and Hiram Itchey shook his head
and every other bone.

When the rebels reached the flag
and pole that Itchey straddled,
although he hungered to be brave,
alas, his brain grew addled.

So Hiram Itchey shouted loud,
"Oh do not shoot me dead!
Shoot, if you must, your country's flag,
but spare my old gray head."

So all Frederick sings today
in praise of Barbara Frietchie,
but no one even will admit
he heard of Hiram Itchey.

An Alto's Lament

I used to be an alto,
and every rounded note
arose and soared in perfect pitch
from my slender throat.

I used to be an alto
before the change set in,
before my firm and fulsome cheeks
fell underneath my chin.

I used to be an alto
before time set its trap;
now most of my anatomy
is sitting on my lap.

So let me sit among the men;
my voice has changed, somehow;
I used to be an alto,
but I'm a tenor now.

Conscience Vs Caution

I adore the friends who see
only the better side of me,
until my conscience, slow to start,
awakens prodding at my heart
for honesty to let them know;
then caution whispers, "Careful—slow!
Expose your faults another day;
even gods have feet of clay.

Almost Made It

The hand of greatness hovered near
the cradle where I lay;
I reached a dimpled, starry fist
to beckon it to stay,
but all my fine persuasive words
got tangled in my throat.
So, thumbs-down, he turned away.
That's how I missed the boat.

Operation Starvation

I did not get a bedtime snack,
and then some plastic snitcher
crept to my room before daylight
and stole my water pitcher.

At breakfast time I drooled and dreamed
of bacon in my bed;
I did not get a steaming tray,
I got a shot instead.

The way my day has gone so far,
more surely than a hunch,
I, in my sleepy post-op state,
will be ignored at lunch.

So take my little gown away,
expose, and cut, and bleed me,
but after you have stitched me up,
please won't somebody feed me?

My Night Before Christmas

T'was the night before Christmas, the tree was aglow,
and outside, the moon lit the new fallen snow;
Sam in his nightshirt and I in my gown,
had just said our prayers, and were settling down,
when out on the lawn rose a racket so dire,
we ran to the door in our nightly attire.
There on the lawn every antler showed clear,
not just one, but a whole bloomin' herd of wild deer!
They were eating my phlox and my rhododendron,
so we whistled and shouted and begged them to run;
then we tore from the tree every pretty, round ball.
We threw them all at them and then, last of all,
Sam unwound the lights that were strung round the tree,
and used them to whip at the rump nearest me.
That buck gave a leap when the cruel deed was done,
and they all raised their heads and they started to run.
And when they were gone, in the first light of day;
we saw all the presents they left on the way.
Sam shouted and moaned, but I said, "Well, my dear,
this should make the grass grow much better next year."

The Wonder Down Under

New Zealanders are Kiwis,
but not the fruit—the bird,
and Maori's are Mowrey's,
  as everyone has heard.

Brisbane doesn't rhyme with pain,
Instead it's called Brisbin,
and Cairns must be pronounced as Cans,
(just like soup comes in).

We are warned, "Don't overtake".
That's what the road signs say;
a body shop's a smash repair
for those who don't 'give way'.

I heard the soccer rules explained.
The Aussies call it fun;
I call it strange, but not as strange
as some things I have done.

I heard an Aborigine
play his didgeridoo;
I rode upon a camel,
and ate a kangaroo.

I parted from down-under land
with much left to explore.
Aussies will say, "Good on you, Mate!"
if I go back for more.

Telly-Ho!

My daughters suffer in their room;
the boys sulk in a tree;
but I approach impending doom
in sweet serenity.

I should be making my escape
by plane, or train, or dugout,
before somebody notices
I pulled the TV plug out.

An If For Under Standing

If I had some mistletoe
to hang above my door,
someone would come along, I know,
to sweep me off the floor.

He'd plant a light and laughing kiss
where kisses make me tingle;
if I had some mistletoe,
how young I'd feel . . . and single.

Sailing On The Amazing Grace

I have a little secret
that I told to quite a few,
but I didn't tell the captain,
and I didn't tell the crew.

I didn't tell the cabin steward
about my awful shame,
but conscience bade me to confess,
and take my share of blame.

You see, way back in Freeport
I made a little slip.
I hadn't been on board an hour
before I broke the ship.

I thought it was a ladder
when I stepped upon that shelf,
and it and I came crashing down;
I didn't hurt myself.

But O humiliation,
when that awful deed was done!
The shelf and I lay on the floor
together, just as one.

After I untwined us,
I gathered up each brace,
I held it in position,
and forced the nails in place.

I used my shoe to pound them
till they tightened on the wall,
then placed the shelf upon them,
and rejoiced it didn't fall.

Then with confession over,
and the consequence to face,
I found the captain, like his ship,
showed me Amazing Grace.

Blanket Verse

I have an independent mind,
and when I try to sleep I find
my mind so filled with poesy
that Morpheus can't conquer me.
Broken spirits, loves that lost,
dreams that toll too high a cost,
lonely spinsters off on sprees,
paths embraced by hemlock trees
softly dripping summer rain,
dance enchantment in my brain.
But when day brings its gift of light,
I lose the visions of the night,
and when I from my bed would creep,
my mind goes blank—I fall asleep.

Prematurely Speaking

I moved the part to center,
and I tried it on the right,
but I can't get that little bit
of silver out of sight.
Perhaps I ought to buy a hat,
or simply yank it out,
or dye it brown, or frost it,
and yet, I have no doubt,
that more would come, so I will keep
that traitor on display,
and find it fascinating
to be *prematurely* gray.

Printed in the United States
33200LVS00005B/226-300

9 781420 857900